Nature's Children

FERRETS

Amanda Harman

GROLIER

FACTS IN BRIEF

Classification of Ferrets

Class:	*Mammalia* (mammals)
Order:	*Carnivora* (meat eaters with specialized teeth)
Family:	*Mustelidae* (weasel family)
Subfamily:	*Mustelinae* (weasels, mink, and polecats)
Genus:	*Mustela* (polecats and ferrets)
Species:	*Mustela nigripes* (black-footed ferret) and *Mustela putorius furo* (common ferret)

World distribution. Black-footed ferrets only in Wyoming; common ferrets throughout the world.

Habitat. Black-footed ferrets in grasslands and partly dry areas on the North American plains; common ferrets as pets.

Distinctive physical characteristics. Long, slim body, short legs, long neck, short snout with whiskers, and rounded ears.

Habits. Black-footed ferrets mostly nocturnal; common ferrets active most often at dusk and dawn.

Diet. Black-footed ferrets feed almost totally on prairie dogs.

© 2004 The Brown Reference Group plc
Printed and bound in U.S.A.
Edited by John Farndon and Angela Koo

Published by:

An imprint of Scholastic Library Publishing Old Sherman Turnpike, Danbury, Connecticut 06816

Library of Congress Cataloging-in-Publication Data
Harman, Amanda, 1968–
    Ferrets / Amanda Harman.
        p. cm. — (Nature's children)
    Includes index.
    Summary: Describes the physical characteristics, habits, and natural environment of ferrets.
    ISBN 0–7172–5957–9 (set)   ISBN 0–7172–5963–3
    1. Ferret—Juvenile literature. [1. Ferret.] I. Title. II. Series.

QL737.C25H365 2004
599.76′628—dc21

2003049167

Contents

Not all hunting animals are big and fierce like lions. Ferrets are small and nippy. In fact, they are so small and nippy that they can chase creatures like rabbits and rats right into their burrows, where they are safe from other hunting animals. The word "ferret" comes from the Latin for "little thief"—and that's just what they are.

There are two kinds of ferret: One comes from North America and the other from Europe. In North America there is a ferret called the black-footed ferret. This ferret is a wild creature that lives on the prairies. It is now one of the rarest of all American animals. European ferrets are called common ferrets. They are entirely tame and are kept by people as pets or to hunt rats and rabbits.

This is one of many black-footed ferrets kept safe in zoos while they are endangered in the wild.

Ferret Bodies

Ferrets are small, furry animals. They are about the size of a small cat, but they have long, thin bodies and short legs—ideal for scurrying down burrows. Their bodies are very bendy too, which is perfect for sliding around tight corners in tunnels. When running above ground, ferrets tend to bound and scamper.

Ferrets have small, beady eyes, small, pointed ears, and a pointed snout with lots of whiskers. They also have sharp teeth and sharp claws—one on each of their five long toes on each foot. At the back ferrets have a long, bushy tail.

Like many hunting animals, ferrets have both their beady eyes facing forward, looking for prey.

Black-footed versus Common

Black-footed and common ferrets are a similar shape, but they look quite different. Black-footed ferrets have buff-colored fur with a light-colored belly. But they also have a brownish head, black feet and legs, and a black tip on the tail—and a black mask across the face. Common ferrets usually have yellowish-white fur all over. Just like pet cats and rats, though, some people breed them to get different fur colors and patterns. They include "Siamese" and "chocolate"-colored ferrets.

Black-footed ferrets are also slightly slimmer and lighter than common ferrets. An adult male black-footed ferret weighs about 1.5 pounds (0.7 kilograms). An adult male common ferret weighs about 2 pounds (1 kilogram). From the tip of its nose to the tip of its tail a black-footed ferret is actually longer than a common ferret—up to 24 inches (61 centimeters). But a lot of this is tail. Its body is pretty much the same length as a common ferret, only slimmer.

Opposite page:
You can tell a black-footed ferret from every other kind of ferret by the black mask across its face.

9

Ferret Relatives

Ferrets belong to a huge family of similar animals called the weasel family, or Mustelidae (said MUST-el-id-eye). There are over 70 different members of the weasel family, including martens, weasels, badgers, and skunks. Most of them are small animals with long bodies and short legs. They are nearly all meat eaters, and they hunt by sight and scent. Although they are small, they are usually very fierce and strong, and can often kill animals that are much bigger than themselves. One of the fiercest is the wolverine, which is no bigger than a dog but can bring down a caribou.

One thing all members of the weasel family have in common is their smell. They all produce a smelly substance called "musk" from underneath their tails. The smelliest of all is the skunk, which sprays its musk at its enemies.

Famed for Fur

Most of the weasel family have lovely, soft fur. That has put them in danger from people who hunt them for their fur, or pelt. Minks and sables have especially beautiful fur. Weasels that live in cold regions, such as stoats, are reddish-brown in summer, but in winter their fur turns pure white. This gorgeous white winter fur is known as ermine and is highly sought after too. For centuries fur trappers have hunted weasels in the wild for their fur. Now minks and many other weasels are often bred for their fur on special farms.

Like other weasels, black-footed and common ferrets both have soft fur that is made up of two layers. A thick layer of short underfur next to the skin keeps the ferrets warm. A waterproof layer of long hairs on the outside keeps water from wetting the fur through. In the past some people farmed common ferrets or hunted black-footed ferrets.

Opposite page:
In winter the stoat's fur turns a beautiful white. This white fur, known as ermine, makes it a target for fur trappers.

Ferret Ancestors

In North America people often call skunks polecats. But in Europe and Asia there is a creature called a polecat that looks almost identical to a common ferret. Common ferrets and European polecats are so alike that scientists think the common ferret is descended from a wild polecat. Polecats and ferrets are almost exactly the same size. The only real difference is that polecats have much darker colored fur. The black-footed ferret is also thought to have descended from a polecat, but a very long time ago.

Polecats live in woods and along riverbanks. They live mainly on the ground, but they climb nimbly and swim well. They hunt at night, feeding mainly on small creatures such as rats and voles—or fish when they can catch them.

Common ferrets come in many different colors.
White ferrets like this are called albinos.

Taming Polecats

Unlike black-footed ferrets, common ferrets are not truly wild. They are all descended from European polecats that were tamed, or "domesticated," long ago. The ancient Romans tamed polecats to drive rabbits, rats, and other pests from underground burrows over 2,000 years ago. The Chinese used them the same way even longer ago. Owners bred special white versions of these polecats, and over the centuries their offspring developed into ferrets.

Common ferrets can rarely survive in the wild for more than a few days. About 120 years ago some ferrets that had mated with polecats were set free in New Zealand to kill off rabbits that farmers thought were pests. The offspring of these ferrets and polecats survived and multiplied. There are now what the locals call ferrets all over New Zealand.

Opposite page:
Black-footed ferrets make their home among the grasses of the prairies of North America.

Prairie Ferrets

Black-footed ferrets are truly wild animals. They make their homes under the grass of the prairies. Here they live closely with little creatures called prairie dogs, their main food.

Once black-footed ferrets roamed far and wide over the plains of North America, from Texas in the south right up to Alberta in western Canada. Experts believe that 200 years ago ferrets lived in 12 different U.S. states and two Canadian provinces, as well as northern Mexico. But as more and more of the prairies have become farmland, the black-footed ferret has become very rare. There are now just small numbers of black-footed ferrets left in the wild. All in all there are even fewer than 1,200, with small colonies in just a few states like Wyoming and South Dakota.

Meat Eaters

Like other members of the weasel family, ferrets are carnivores, which means that they eat meat.

Black-footed ferrets live almost entirely by killing and eating one animal, a small squirrel-like creature called a prairie dog. A black-footed ferret eats an entire prairie dog every three or four days. Occasionally ferrets eat other small animals, such as rabbits, mice, birds, lizards, and even insects. But it is the prairie dog that is their favorite meal by far.

All ferrets are keen hunters. This common ferret is dragging away a rabbit it has killed.

Ferrets and Prairie Dogs

Opposite page:
Prairie dogs are not dogs at all, but rodents that live on the prairie. They get their name from the doglike "yip-yip" sound they make.

Few hunting animals rely quite so much on one kind of prey as black-footed ferrets do on prairie dogs. In fact, the ferrets sometimes live in the same hole as prairie dogs.

Prairie dogs are not dogs at all but squirrels that live on the ground on the prairies and feed on plants. They are amazingly sociable little animals. Thousands of them live together in a vast network of burrows called a "town."

Prairie dog towns are so big that all kinds of other creatures often move in and squat, from deer mice to salamanders. Prairie dogs escape from large animals and birds by darting into their burrows, but some of the squatters are just as dangerous. Many prairie dogs fall victim to a nasty meeting in the dark with a badger or a prairie rattlesnake. The most ferocious of the squatters, though, is the black-footed ferret.

Keen Hunters

Black-footed ferrets are skillful hunters of prairie dogs. They use all their senses for detecting their victims. To see and hear better, they often sit up on their back legs. They look out for small movements and listen carefully for any sounds in the grass that might reveal a prairie dog on the move. But it is their acute sense of smell they rely on most of all. Even when a prairie dog is quite far away, a ferret can sniff it out by following the slight scent the dogs leave behind.

Once they sniff out a group of prairie dogs, ferrets try to sneak as close as they can. They scamper silently through the grass until near enough to pounce. If lucky, a ferret can make a quick killing without too much trouble.

Squeezing into Burrows

Prairie dogs work together to avoid being caught by enemies. Whenever a group goes above ground to forage for food, one sits upright, watching and listening for danger. At the first sign of trouble, such as a ferret on the prowl, it lets out an alarm call to warn the others in the group. The alarm call is a little bark, which is why these animals are called prairie "dogs."

As soon as other prairie dogs hear the alarm call, they scatter as fast as they can and dash underground. The ferret follows, running speedily in pursuit. The prairie dogs are not safe even in their burrows. The ferret's long, flexible body is perfect for squeezing down the underground tunnels after them.

Killing Tools

Once a ferret has caught a prairie dog or a rabbit, it kills it quickly and easily. Like other carnivores, the ferret is equipped with lots of excellent tools for the job.

It grips onto the animal's body with its large claws and bites the back of its neck with its powerful jaws and jabbing teeth. Just one bite into the animal's skull is usually enough to kill it. Then the ferret uses other teeth as sharp as razors for slicing through the flesh.

Black-footed ferrets need to eat lots of food to survive and grow properly. They have to catch and kill at least two prairie dogs a week.

Black-footed ferrets have very strong jaws and sharp teeth— perfect for killing a prairie dog.

Nighttime Hunters

Sometimes black-footed ferrets hunt during the day, when prairie dogs are up and about feeding. But most of the time they hunt at night. Animals that are active mainly after dark are called nocturnal.

At night prairie dogs are asleep in their burrows deep underground. So a ferret uses its excellent sense of smell to tell which burrows are occupied. When it sniffs out a sleeping dog, it slithers quickly down the tunnel to kill its prey, often before the prairie dogs even have a chance to wake up. But prairie dogs do not always die without a struggle. Many fight back, attacking the ferret's neck and face with their claws and teeth.

Black-footed ferrets prefer to do their hunting at night, when prairie dogs are sleeping underground.

Male and female black-footed ferrets get together to mate in the springtime.

Ferret Kits

Unlike prairie dogs, black-footed ferrets prefer to be on their own. They do not live in groups for most of the time. Once a ferret reaches one year old, however, it is ready to have young of its own. In March or April males and females seek each other out and get together to mate. Then they part again immediately after. A month and a half later the female gives birth to a litter of babies.

The baby ferrets are born in a burrow underground and are called "kits." There are usually between three and five kits in a litter. Each kit weighs a tiny fraction of an ounce (5–9 grams) and is completely dependent on its mom when it is born. Its eyes are closed, and it has a covering of thin white hair over its body. It gets all its food by sucking its mom's milk. This is called suckling.

Growing Ferrets

Opposite page:
Ferrets are very agile and fast on their feet. They learn their agility in the games they play as kits.

Ferret kits finally open their eyes when they are about three weeks old. Soon they may even crawl up the tunnel and pop their heads above ground for a peek at the world. But they are still totally dependent on their mother and go on suckling until they are around 12 weeks old. Gradually, though, they begin to eat more and more of the meat mom brings back for them. Soon they are ready to stay above ground for longer.

Ferret kits are very playful. They wrestle each other to the ground and roll over and over. They practice all the skills they will need later to be excellent hunters. One type of play is known as the "ferret dance." For this the kits hop backward with their mouths open and their backs arched.

A male black-footed ferret fiercely defends his own patch against intruders.

Marking Territories

By the end of the summer the young ferrets are old enough to hunt for their own food. They leave their mother and brothers and sisters, and set out to live alone.

Each ferret sets up its own area of land that it travels through in search of food. This area is called a territory. The territories of female ferrets never overlap, but the males' territories are much larger and may contain those of several female ferrets.

Black-footed ferrets guard their territories jealously. They attack any other ferrets that enter, apart from their mates during the breeding time or their youngsters. To make sure other ferrets do not enter their territory by accident, the ferrets mark out the edges. They do this with dung containing the smelly musk from under their tail. Each ferret has its own particular smell.

On the Lookout

Ferrets might be excellent hunters, but they have their own predators, too. During the day they must be on the lookout for other carnivores such as hawks and foxes that hunt them. At night owls are their worst enemies. There are fewer predators out and about at night, however. That is one of the reasons why ferrets prefer to be nocturnal most of the time.

Ferrets make a wide range of sounds. When they are faced with an enemy, they hiss or make a loud chattering call. This warns their kits to run for safety in the burrow. Females also make whining noises to communicate with their young.

If it emerges from its burrow during the day, a black-footed ferret has to keep a sharp lookout for danger.

Fun Pets

Common ferrets are becoming more and more popular as pets in the United States. They are playful and friendly animals. They are very intelligent and clean, too. They can even be taught tricks and to use a litter tray. Some owners enter their pets into competitions at ferret shows. There are prizes for the healthiest ferrets and the ones with the most beautiful coat colors and patterns.

However, it is still against the law to keep ferrets as pets in the states of California and Hawaii. There are restrictions on owning ferrets in some other places, such as New York.

Common ferrets make attractive pets. This is an albino (white) common ferret mother with its young.

On the Way Out

Opposite page: *Black-footed ferrets survive by hunting prairie dogs. When farmers drove prairie dogs off the prairies, they threatened the survival of the ferret.*

Prairie dogs once lived over most of the prairies. But as the prairies were plowed for farmland, their natural homes were destroyed. The prairie dogs were also poisoned by farmers. The farmers said they were pests because they ate the same food as their cattle and dug holes that cattle and horses could stumble over. Driven from their homes and poisoned, prairie dogs dwindled drastically in number, and now only a few pockets of survivors are left.

As the prairie dog suffered, so did its main hunter, the black-footed ferret. A few ferrets were killed directly by eating poisoned prairie dogs. But most of them starved to death as their prey slowly vanished or were, like the prairie dogs, left with nowhere to live. By the 1960s the only group of ferrets that seemed to be left was a small colony in southwestern South Dakota.

The End of the Ferret?

In 1979 the last surviving ferret from the southwestern South Dakota colony died. Scientists thought it was the last ferret, and so they were officially said to be extinct.

Then in 1981 a dead black-footed ferret was found, killed by a ranch dog in northwestern Wyoming. Scientists immediately investigated. Three years later they found a small group of 130 or so ferrets in nearby Meeteetse in Wyoming. They began studying the ferrets to learn about their habits.

Sadly, the ferrets were soon all but wiped out again, as a disease called sylvatic plague struck down both prairie dogs and ferrets. To save the last 18 wild black-footed ferrets, the scientists took them into captivity in 1987.

Back from the Brink

Scientists spread the captive ferrets out among various different zoos and breeding centers—so that if disaster struck one group, another might survive. The scientists hoped to breed these captive ferrets and reintroduce their kits into the wild.

The first little group was set free in Wyoming in 1991. A few years later more were set free in Montana and South Dakota. By 1999, 1,185 ferrets had been released in various places. Many have died since they were set free, but a few have survived to have their own kits in the wild. And in the future more will be released.

By the year 2010 the scientists hope there could be as many as 1,500 ferrets living wild once more on the North American plains. Crucially the scientists hope each colony will include 30 breeding pairs—males and females able to have a family of kits in the wild. If that happens, the black-footed ferret will no longer be in danger.

Words to Know

Breed To produce young.

Camouflage Patterns or colors that help an animal blend in with its surroundings.

Carnivore An animal that eats meat.

Domestication The taming and breeding of an animal or plant to live with humans and be useful to them.

Endangered When an animal is in danger of becoming extinct.

Extinct When all the animals of a particular species have died, and there are no more left anywhere in the world.

Feral A domesticated animal that has escaped or has been released into the world.

Mammal A warm-blooded animal that is covered by hair or fur, gives birth to live young, and produces milk to feed them.

Mate To come together to produce young.

Nocturnal An animal that is mainly active at night.

Predator An animal that hunts and eats other animals for food.

Prey An animal that another animal hunts for food.

Rodent Any of the group of animals with front teeth, especially used for gnawing.

Species A particular type of animal.

Territory An area where an animal hunts or breeds.

INDEX

Cover Photo: Bruce Coleman: Stephen C. Kaufman
Photo Credits: Ardea: Ian Beames 20, Edgar T. Jones 31, Ken Lucas 8; **Bruce Coleman:**
Jeff Foott 19, Steven C. Kaufman 4, Hans Reinhard 11; **Corbis:** D. Robert & Lorri Franz 35,
39, 43, Jeff Vanuga 7, 45; **NHPA:** Mark Bowler 28, Gerard Lacz 40, Michael Leach 16;
Oxford Scientific Films: Alan & Sandy Carey 24/25, Mark Hamblin 15, Breck P. Kent/AA 12,
Barbara Reed/AA 32, Wendy Shattil & Bob Rozinski 36; **Still Pictures:** Patricio Robles Gil 23.